Cross Stitch

Christmas Stockings

2

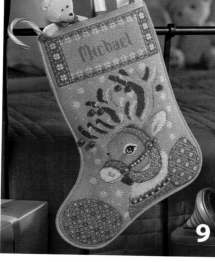

9

16

22

28

Deck the halls with Christmas stockings!

LEISURE ARTS, INC. • Maumelle, Arkansas

1

Wintry Blue Santa Stocking

Capture St. Nick on his midnight travels by stitching this spectacular stocking.

Designed by Donna Vermillion Giampa

Stitch Count= 145w × 219h

FABRIC SIZE
• One 18" × 24" (45.7cm × 61.0cm) piece of 28-ct. Bluebell Hand-Dyed Jobelan® by Wichelt Imports (stitched over two threads)

DESIGN SIZE
• 28-ct. = 10³/₈" × 15⁵/₈" (26.4cm × 39.7cm)

FINISHING MATERIALS
• ¹/₃ yard of light blue velveteen
• ¹/₃ yard of cotton fabric for lining
• 1¼ yards of ¼"-wide off-white cording
• Matching sewing thread

GENERAL INSTRUCTIONS
Center the design and begin stitching over two fabric threads. Work blended cross stitches with one strand of cotton embroidery floss and one strand of Kreinik blending filament. Work all other cross stitches, three-quarter stitches, half cross stitches, and quarter stitches with two strands of cotton embroidery floss or DMC® Light Effects floss. Use one strand of Light Effects floss to work French knots. Work backstitches with one strand of cotton embroidery floss or Light Effects floss. *Note*: The gray dashed line on the chart indicates the stocking shape for finishing purposes only; do not stitch. Using the alphabet on page 8, personalize the stocking with the desired name, making sure to center the name on the cuff. Use a pressing cloth to carefully iron the needlework from the back before finishing.

FINISHING INSTRUCTIONS
Use a ½" seam allowance for all seams unless otherwise noted. Trim the needlework to within ½" outside the gray dashed line. With the wrong side up, use this piece as a template to cut one back piece from the right side of the velveteen and one piece from the right side of the lining fabric. Flip the needlework right side up and use it as a template to cut one piece from the right side of the lining fabric. With right sides together, sew the stocking front to the velveteen back, leaving the top open. Turn the stocking right side out and iron using a pressing cloth. Sew the lining pieces together in the same manner as the stocking, but leave a 4" opening along the bottom of the "foot" for turning as well. Leave the lining wrong side out and insert the stocking into the lining, aligning the top edges. Pin in place.

Sew all the way around the top, stitching through all layers. Begin pulling the toe of the stocking through the opening in the lining and continue pulling until the entire stocking and lining are right side out. By hand, neatly slipstitch the opening in the lining closed. Tuck the lining inside the stocking and press. Hand-sew the cording around the edge of the stocking, tucking the cut edges into the top of the stocking at the beginning and end. Create a small hanging loop by cutting a 1¾" × 5" strip from leftover fabric. Fold in half along the length with right sides together and press. Sew along the cut edge, turn right sides out, and fold in half to form a loop. Attach to the top left corner of the stocking with a few hand-stitches.

Note: Please read all instructions on page 32 before beginning.

CROSS STITCH

ANCHOR		DMC	COLOR
002	·	White	White
148	A	311	Medium Navy Blue
979	J	312	Very Dark Baby Blue
978	N	322	Dark Baby Blue
977	U	334	Medium Baby Blue
933	e	543	Ultra Very Light Beige Brown
903	L	640	Very Dark Beige Gray
392	C	642	Dark Beige Gray
830	E	644	Medium Beige Gray
926	H	712	Cream
1022	4	760	Salmon
1021	m	761	Light Salmon
128	8	775	Very Light Baby Blue
390	Z	822	Light Beige Gray
381	V	938	Ultra Dark Coffee Brown
905	Y	3021	Very Dark Brown Gray
883	h	3064	Desert Sand
129	T	3325	Light Baby Blue
1037	6	3756	Ultra Very Light Baby Blue

CROSS STITCH

ANCHOR		DMC	COLOR
1009	3	3770	Very Light Tawny
1007	K	3772	Very Dark Desert Sand
1008	7	3773	Medium Desert Sand
778	2	3774	Very Light Desert Sand
273	M	3787	Dark Brown Gray
9159	S	3841	Pale Baby Blue
358	G	3862	Dark Mocha Beige
379	D	3863	Medium Mocha Beige
376	b	3864	Light Mocha Beige

DMC LIGHT EFFECTS		COLOR
E168	B	Silver

CROSS STITCH WITH BLENDED THREAD

KREINIK BLENDING FILAMENT		ANCHOR	DMC	COLOR
	F	002	White	White
032				Pearl

FRENCH KNOT

DMC LIGHT EFFECTS		COLOR
E168	•	Silver

BACKSTITCH

ANCHOR		DMC	COLOR
148	—	311	Medium Navy Blue
979	—	312	Very Dark Baby Blue
401	—	413	Dark Pewter Gray
936	—	632	Ultra Very Dark Desert Sand
381	—	938	Ultra Dark Coffee Brown
152	—	939	Very Dark Navy Blue
905	—	3021	Very Dark Brown Gray
273	—	3787	Dark Brown Gray

DMC LIGHT EFFECTS		COLOR
E168	—	Silver

▦ Gray area indicates last row of previous section of design.

3

Note: Use alphabet on page 8 to chart and center desired name on cuff area.

CROSS STITCH

ANCHOR		DMC	COLOR
002	·	White	White
148	A	311	Medium Navy Blue
979	J	312	Very Dark Baby Blue
978	N	322	Dark Baby Blue
977	U	334	Medium Baby Blue
933	e	543	Ultra Very Light Beige Brown
903	L	640	Very Dark Beige Gray
392	C	642	Dark Beige Gray
830	E	644	Medium Beige Gray
926	H	712	Cream
1022	4	760	Salmon
1021	m	761	Light Salmon
128	8	775	Very Light Baby Blue
390	Z	822	Light Beige Gray
381	V	938	Ultra Dark Coffee Brown
905	Y	3021	Very Dark Brown Gray
883	h	3064	Desert Sand
129	T	3325	Light Baby Blue
1037	6	3756	Ultra Very Light Baby Blue
1009	3	3770	Very Light Tawny
1007	K	3772	Very Dark Desert Sand
1008	7	3773	Medium Desert Sand
778	2	3774	Very Light Desert Sand
273	M	3787	Dark Brown Gray
9159	S	3841	Pale Baby Blue
358	G	3862	Dark Mocha Beige
379	D	3863	Medium Mocha Beige
376	b	3864	Light Mocha Beige
DMC LIGHT EFFECTS			COLOR
E168	B		Silver

CROSS STITCH WITH BLENDED THREAD

KREINIK BLENDING FILAMENT		ANCHOR	DMC	COLOR
	F	002	White	White
032				Pearl

FRENCH KNOT

DMC LIGHT EFFECTS		COLOR
E168	·	Silver

BACKSTITCH

ANCHOR		DMC	COLOR
148	——	311	Medium Navy Blue
979	——	312	Very Dark Baby Blue
401	——	413	Dark Pewter Gray
936	——	632	Ultra Very Dark Desert Sand
381	——	938	Ultra Dark Coffee Brown
152	——	939	Very Dark Navy Blue
905	——	3021	Very Dark Brown Gray
273	——	3787	Dark Brown Gray
DMC LIGHT EFFECTS		COLOR
E168	——	Silver

Gray area indicates last row of previous section of design.

Chart Layout

A	B
C	D

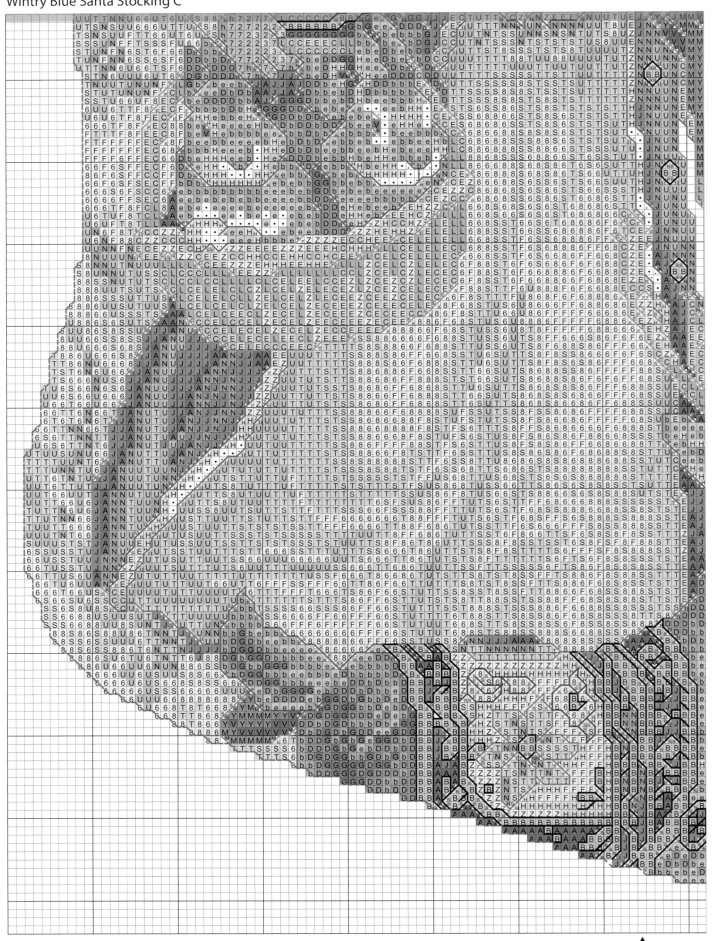

CHART LAYOUT

| A | B |
| C | D |

Note: Color key can be found on page 5.

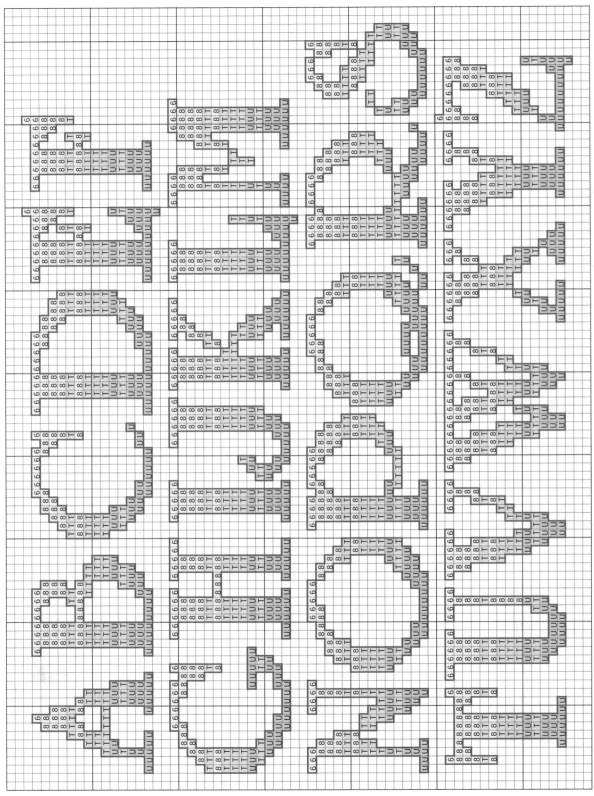

Note: Color key can be found on page 5.

Reindeer Stocking

Designed by Barbara Sestok

Loved ones will be thrilled to receive something made by you for the holidays, like this reindeer stocking. Filled with goodies, it's the perfect way to start Christmas Day!

Stitch Count = 135w × 198h

FABRIC SIZE
• One 18" × 22" (45.7cm × 55.9cm) piece of 28-ct. Dusty Green Jobelan® by Wichelt Imports (stitched over two threads)

DESIGN SIZE
• 28-ct. = 9⅝" × 14⅛" (24.4cm × 35.9cm)

EMBELLISHMENTS
• Old Gold #05557 pebble beads by Mill Hill®
• 7 red jingle bells, 10mm

FINISHING MATERIALS
• 1 yard of cotton fabric for backing and lining
• 1½ yards of ¼"-wide cording
• Matching sewing thread

GENERAL INSTRUCTIONS
Center the design and begin stitching over two fabric threads. Work cross stitches and French knots with two strands of cotton embroidery floss or two strands of DMC® Light Effects floss. Work backstitches with one strand of DMC 433/Anchor 358 or two strands of DMC 3852/Anchor 306. *Note*: Do not stitch the outline around the stocking, as it is the finishing guideline. Using the alphabet on page 11, personalize the stocking with the desired name, making sure to center the name on the cuff. Use a pressing cloth to carefully iron the needlework from the back before adding embellishments. Attach pebble beads with two strands of matching floss. Attach jingle bells to ends of backstitch "strings" on antlers with one strand of matching floss before finishing.

FINISHING INSTRUCTIONS
Trim the needlework to within 1" outside the edge of the stitching. With the wrong side up, use this piece as a template to cut two stocking shapes from the right side of the cotton fabric (one will be for the backing, the other for half of the lining). Flip the needlework right side up and use as a template to cut one piece from the right side of the lining fabric.

Cut and piece together enough 1½"-wide bias strips of fabric to form one strip 40" long. (The photographed model used leftover needlework fabric, but you may use a coordinating fabric if you do not have enough extra needlework fabric.) Fold the fabric strip over the cording, with

the long edges together and right side out. Using a zipper foot, sew close to the cording through both layers to form the piping. Pin piping around the stocking front, making sure the cording is flush with the edge of the stitching. (Use the finishing line on the chart for reference.) Using a zipper foot, sew the piping around the perimeter of the stocking front, making sure to sew as close to the cording as possible.

With right sides together, sew the stocking front to the backing piece, sewing tight to the cording, but leaving the top open. Trim the side and bottom seam allowances to ¼". Turn the stocking right side out and iron using a pressing cloth. Sew the lining pieces together in the same manner as the stocking, but use a 1" seam allowance and leave a 4" opening along the bottom of the "foot" for turning. Trim the side and bottom seam allowances to ¼". Leave the lining wrong side out and insert the stocking into the lining, aligning the top edges. Pin in place. Sew all the way around the top along the edge of the stitching, sewing through all layers. Begin pulling the toe of the stocking through the opening in the lining and continue pulling until the entire stocking and lining are right side out. By hand, neatly slipstitch the opening in the lining closed. Tuck the lining inside the stocking and press.

Create a small hanging loop by cutting a 1¾" × 5" strip from leftover needlework fabric. Fold in half along the length with right sides together and press. Sew along the cut edge, turn right side out, and fold in half to form a loop. Attach the hanging loop to the top right corner of the stocking with a few hand-stitches.

CROSS STITCH

ANCHOR		DMC	COLOR
002	•	White	White
979	H	312	Very Dark Baby Blue
1025	B	347	Very Dark Salmon
006	C	353	Peach
1014	a	355	Dark Terra Cotta
1046	W	435	Very Light Brown
1045	b	436	Tan
933	<	543	Ultra Very Light Beige Brown
046	F	666	Bright Christmas Red
886	>	677	Very Light Old Gold
226	S	702	Kelly Green
256	U	704	Bright Chartreuse
305	2	728	Topaz
275	4	746	Off White
380	e	779	Dark Cocoa
257	Y	905	Dark Parrot Green
268	R	3345	Dark Hunter Green
382	r	3371	Black Brown
306	8	3852	Very Dark Straw
379	m	3863	Medium Mocha Beige
376	6	3864	Light Mocha Beige

DMC LIGHT EFFECTS		COLOR
E5200	L	White

FRENCH KNOT

ANCHOR		DMC	COLOR
306	•	3852	Very Dark Straw

BACKSTITCH

ANCHOR		DMC	COLOR
358	——	433	Medium Brown
306	——	3852	Very Dark Straw

EMBELLISHMENTS

MILL HILL PEBBLE	BEAD	COLOR
05557	●	Old Gold

10MM JINGLE BELL		COLOR
	●	Red

▨ Gray area indicates last row of previous section of design.

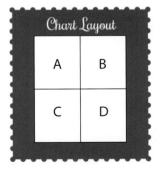

Chart Layout

A	B
C	D

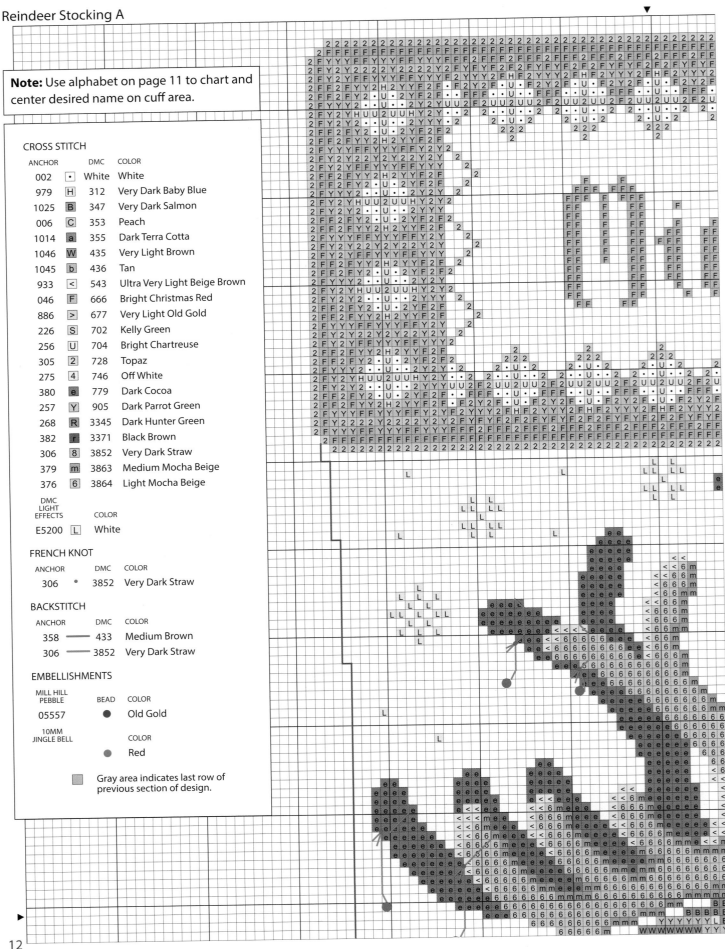

Note: Use alphabet on page 11 to chart and center desired name on cuff area.

CROSS STITCH

ANCHOR	DMC	COLOR	
002	· White	White	
979	H	312	Very Dark Baby Blue
1025	B	347	Very Dark Salmon
006	C	353	Peach
1014	a	355	Dark Terra Cotta
1046	W	435	Very Light Brown
1045	b	436	Tan
933	<	543	Ultra Very Light Beige Brown
046	F	666	Bright Christmas Red
886	>	677	Very Light Old Gold
226	S	702	Kelly Green
256	U	704	Bright Chartreuse
305	2	728	Topaz
275	4	746	Off White
380	e	779	Dark Cocoa
257	Y	905	Dark Parrot Green
268	R	3345	Dark Hunter Green
382	r	3371	Black Brown
306	8	3852	Very Dark Straw
379	m	3863	Medium Mocha Beige
376	6	3864	Light Mocha Beige

DMC LIGHT EFFECTS		COLOR	
E5200	L	White	

FRENCH KNOT

ANCHOR	DMC	COLOR	
306	·	3852	Very Dark Straw

BACKSTITCH

ANCHOR	DMC	COLOR	
358	——	433	Medium Brown
306	——	3852	Very Dark Straw

EMBELLISHMENTS

MILL HILL PEBBLE	BEAD	COLOR	
05557	●	Old Gold	

10MM JINGLE BELL		COLOR	
	●	Red	

Gray area indicates last row of previous section of design.

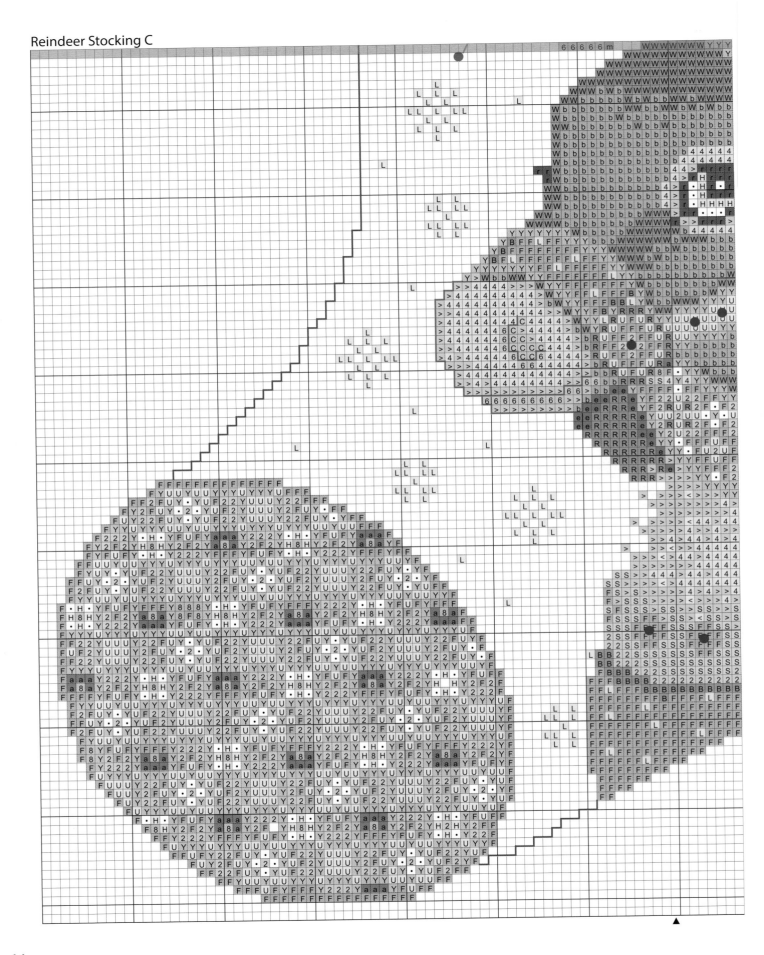

Reindeer Stocking D

Note: Color key can be found on page 12.

Winter Magic Stocking

Add a little magic to your home with this Christmas stocking! The lighthearted design featuring elves building a snowman is sure to bring charm to the holiday season.

Designed by Michele Johnson

Stitch Count = 146w × 214h

FABRIC SIZE
• One 17" × 21" (43.2cm × 53.3cm) piece of 14-ct. white aida

DESIGN SIZE
• 14-ct. = 10½" × 15¼" (26.7cm × 38.7cm)

FINISHING MATERIALS
• ⅓ yard of fabric for backing
• ⅓ yard of fabric for lining
• 1¼ yards of white cording
• Matching sewing thread

GENERAL INSTRUCTIONS
Center the design and begin stitching. Work cross stitches and quarter stitches with two strands of cotton embroidery floss. Work blended cross stitches with two strands of cotton embroidery floss and one strand of Kreinik blending filament. Use one strand of cotton embroidery floss to work backstitches. *Note:* The red line on the chart indicates the stocking shape for finishing purposes only; do not stitch. Using the alphabet on page 17, personalize the stocking with the desired name using two strands of cotton embroidery floss, making sure to center the name on the cuff. Use a pressing cloth to carefully iron the needlework from the back before finishing.

FINISHING INSTRUCTIONS
If your backing fabric has a distinctive nap to it, align the fabric with the length of the stocking so the nap is laying properly. Pin around the stocking shape and cut fabric to the size of the needlework. Sew the needlework and the backing fabric together along the edge of the needlework (by hand or sewing machine) and then trim both the needlework and excess backing fabric to within approximately ½" from the design. Clip the seam allowance approximately every ½" and slightly closer together around the curved areas. (This allows for a smooth shape around the curves of the stocking.) Do not cut into the needlework.

Fold the lining material over with right sides together. Place the stocking down on the wrong side of the lining and pin. Trace the exact shape of the stocking onto the lining, including the seam allowance. Cut the stocking shape from the lining material. Sew the lining together, leaving a ½" seam allowance and a 3" unsewn space between the toe and the heel. Clip the seam allowance on the lining.

Insert the lining into the stocking with right sides together. Pin and sew the top of the lining to the top of the stocking. Turn the stocking right side out and pull the lining out. Pin and sew the opening in the foot. Place the lining back inside the stocking. (*Note:* You may want to tack the toe of the stocking with a couple of stitches to keep the lining secured.) Attach cording by hand-sewing the underside of it to the edge of the stocking. (Invisible thread hides any signs of stitches.) Attach cording to the top right corner of the stocking for a hanger.

Chart Layout

A	B
C	D

CROSS STITCH

ANCHOR		DMC	COLOR
1026	◇	225	Ultra Very Light Shell Pink
1006	A	304	Medium Christmas Red
978	G	322	Dark Baby Blue
977	8	334	Medium Baby Blue
117	5	341	Light Blue Violet
235	C	414	Dark Steel Gray
398	◉	415	Pearl Gray
310	V	434	Light Brown
1045	7	436	Tan
099	H	552	Medium Violet
096	4	554	Light Violet
167	3	598	Light Turquoise
046	?	666	Bright Christmas Red
326	Z	720	Dark Orange Spice
324	∧	721	Medium Orange Spice
323	⊡	722	Light Orange Spice

CROSS STITCH

ANCHOR		DMC	COLOR
305	#	725	Medium Light Topaz
361	6	738	Very Light Tan
301	U	744	Pale Yellow
234	⊙	762	Very Light Pearl Gray
307	L	783	Medium Topaz
176	N	793	Medium Cornflower Blue
359	π	801	Dark Coffee Brown
168	F	807	Peacock Blue
923	B	909	Very Dark Emerald Green
209	R	912	Light Emerald Green
129	E	3325	Light Baby Blue
035	◁	3705	Dark Melon
120	⊘	3747	Very Light Blue Violet
1031	Y	3753	Ultra Very Light Antique Blue
868	T	3779	Very Light Terra Cotta
236	S	3799	Very Dark Pewter Gray

CROSS STITCH WITH BLENDED THREAD

KREINIK BLENDING FILAMENT		ANCHOR	DMC	COLOR
032	☆	002	White	White Pearl
032	⊠	129	3325	Light Baby Blue Pearl
032	◮	1031	3753	Ultra Very Light Antique Blue Pearl

BACKSTITCH

ANCHOR		DMC	COLOR
403	——	310	Black
978	——	322	Dark Baby Blue

Gray area indicates last row of previous section of design.

Note: Please read all instructions on page 32 before beginning.

Note: Use alphabet on page 17 to chart and center desired name on cuff area.

CROSS STITCH

ANCHOR		DMC	COLOR
1026	◇	225	Ultra Very Light Shell Pink
1006	A	304	Medium Christmas Red
978	G	322	Dark Baby Blue
977	8	334	Medium Baby Blue
117	5	341	Light Blue Violet
235	C	414	Dark Steel Gray
398	◎	415	Pearl Gray
310	V	434	Light Brown
1045	7	436	Tan
099	H	552	Medium Violet
096	4	554	Light Violet
167	3	598	Light Turquoise
046	?	666	Bright Christmas Red
326	Z	720	Dark Orange Spice
324	∧	721	Medium Orange Spice
323	⊡	722	Light Orange Spice
305	#	725	Medium Light Topaz
361	6	738	Very Light Tan
301	U	744	Pale Yellow
234	⊙	762	Very Light Pearl Gray
307	L	783	Medium Topaz
176	N	793	Medium Cornflower Blue
359	π	801	Dark Coffee Brown
168	F	807	Peacock Blue
923	B	909	Very Dark Emerald Green
209	R	912	Light Emerald Green
129	E	3325	Light Baby Blue
035	<	3705	Dark Melon
120	○	3747	Very Light Blue Violet
1031	Y	3753	Ultra Very Light Antique Blue
868	T	3779	Very Light Terra Cotta
236	$	3799	Very Dark Pewter Gray

CROSS STITCH WITH BLENDED THREAD

KREINIK BLENDING FILAMENT		ANCHOR	DMC	COLOR
	☆	002	White	White
032				Pearl
	⊠	129	3325	Light Baby Blue
032				Pearl
	⌇	1031	3753	Ultra Very Light Antique Blue
032				Pearl

BACKSTITCH

ANCHOR		DMC	COLOR
403	▬	310	Black
978	▬	322	Dark Baby Blue
	▦		Gray area indicates last row of previous section of design.

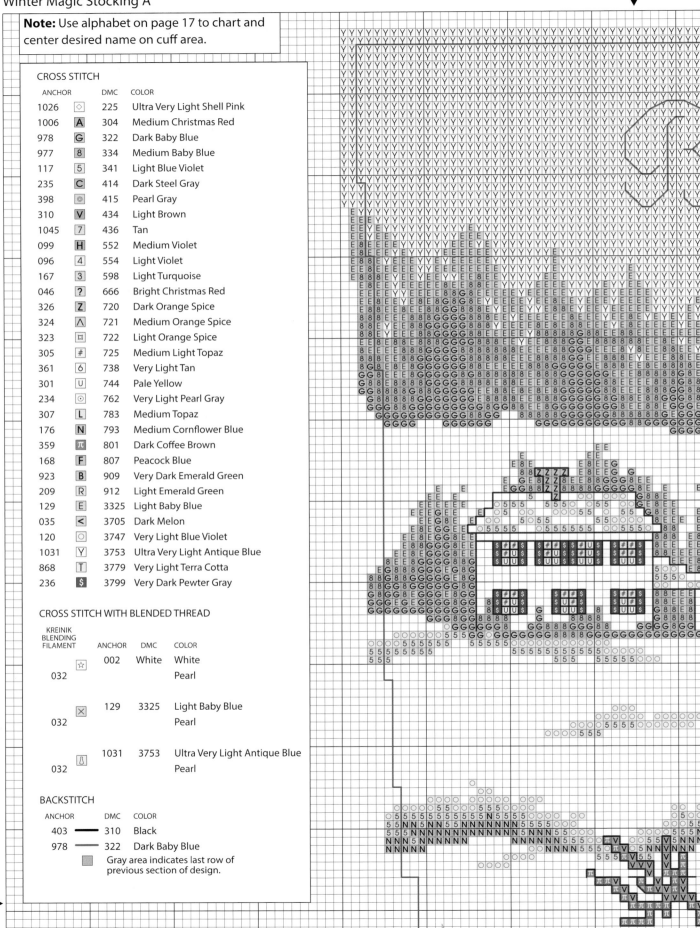

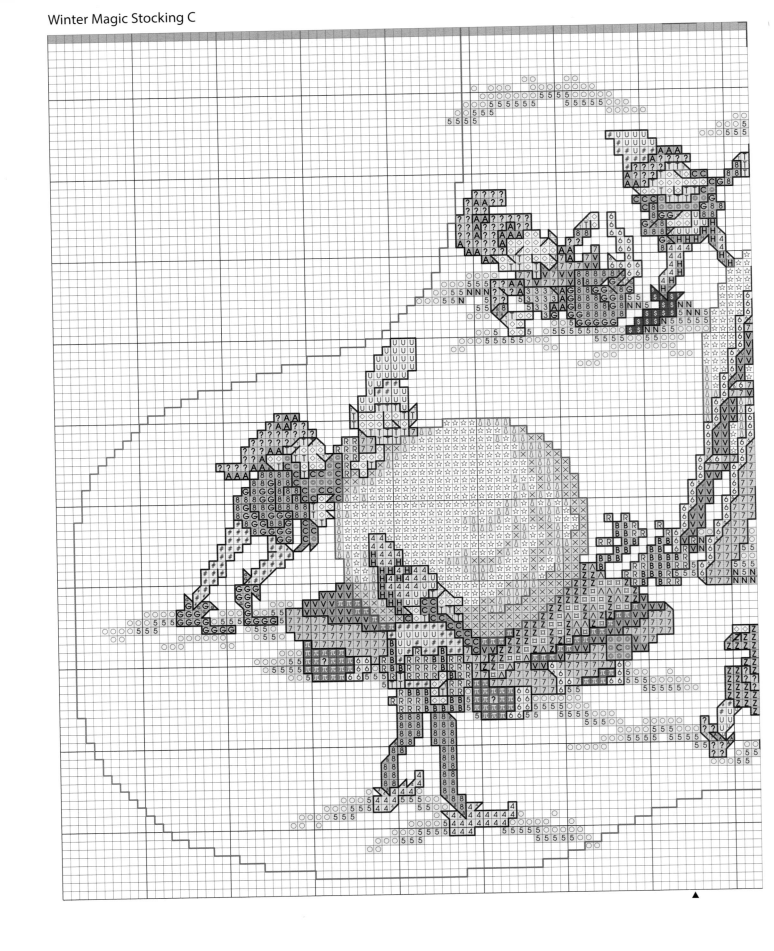

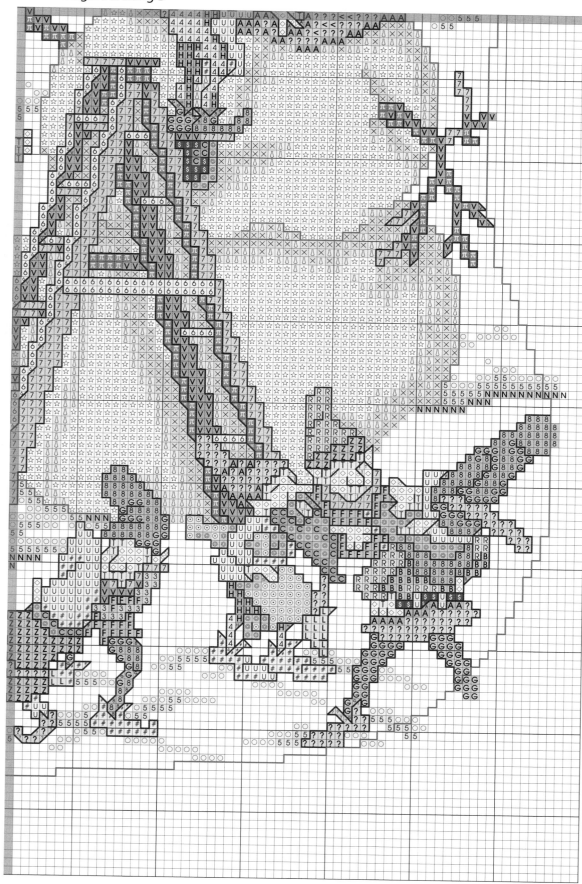

Note: Color key can be found on page 18.

Poinsettia Stocking

What is Christmas without a cross stitch design featuring our favorite holiday flower? This elegant stocking looks stunning displayed on a fireplace mantel.

Designed by Barbara Sestok

Stitch Count = 138w × 212h

FABRIC SIZE
- One 17" × 21" (43.2cm × 53.3cm) piece of 32-ct. Tumbleweed 100% Linen by Wichelt Imports (stitched over two threads)

DESIGN SIZE
- 32-ct. = 8⅝" × 13¼" (21.9cm × 33.7cm)

FINISHING MATERIALS
- 1 yard of black cotton fabric for backing and lining
- 1½ yards of ¼"-diameter cording
- Matching sewing thread

GENERAL INSTRUCTIONS
Center the design and begin stitching over two fabric threads. Work cross stitches with two strands of cotton embroidery floss and French knots with one strand of cotton embroidery floss. *Note:* Do not stitch the outline around the stocking, as it is the finishing guideline. Use a pressing cloth to carefully iron the needlework from the back before finishing.

FINISHING INSTRUCTIONS
Trim the needlework to within 1" of the stitching, referring to the finishing guideline as necessary. With the wrong side up, use this as a template to cut out two stocking shapes from the right side of the cotton fabric (one for the backing and one for half of the lining). Flip the needlework right side up and use as a template to cut one piece from the right side of the cotton fabric for the other half of the lining.

Cut and piece together enough 1½"-wide bias strips of fabric to form one 36"-long strip. Fold the fabric strip over the cording, with the long edges together and right side out. Using a zipper foot, sew close to the cording through both layers to form the piping. Pin the piping around the stocking front, making sure the cording is flush with the edge of the stitching. Using a zipper foot, sew the piping around the sides and bottom of the stocking front, making sure to sew as close to the cording as possible.

With right sides together, sew the stocking front to the backing piece, sewing tight to the outside of the cording but leaving the top open. Trim the side and bottom seam allowances to ¼". Turn the stocking right side out and iron using a pressing cloth. Sew the lining pieces together in the same manner as the stocking, but use a 1" seam allowance and leave a 4" opening along the bottom of the "foot" for turning. Trim the side and bottom seam allowances to ¼". Leave the lining wrong side out and insert the stocking into the lining, matching up the top edges. Pin in place. Sew all the way around the top, ⅛" from the edge of the stitching, sewing through all layers.

Begin pulling the toe of the stocking through the opening in the lining and continue pulling until the entire stocking and lining are right side out. By hand, neatly slipstitch the opening in the lining closed. Tuck the lining inside the stocking, leaving ¼" of lining showing at top; press. Create a small hanging loop by cutting a 1½" × 5" strip from leftover black cotton fabric. Fold in half lengthwise with right sides together and press. Tuck in the edges ¼" and press. Topstitch with a ⅛" seam allowance. Fold in half to form a loop. Attach to the top right corner of the stocking with a few hand-stitches.

Note: Please read all instructions on page 32 before beginning.

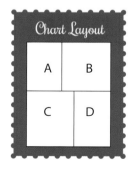

Chart Layout

A	B
C	D

Gray area indicates last row of previous section of design.

CROSS STITCH

ANCHOR		DMC	COLOR
1006	O	304	Medium Christmas Red
403	X	310	Black
1025	A	347	Very Dark Salmon
334	C	606	Bright Orange Red
046	H	666	Bright Christmas Red
305	L	728	Topaz
309	G	781	Very Dark Topaz
307	S	783	Medium Topaz
043	U	815	Medium Garnet
390	B	822	Light Beige Gray
333	R	900	Dark Burnt Orange
332	E	946	Medium Burnt Orange

FRENCH KNOT

ANCHOR		DMC	COLOR
906	•	829	Very Dark Golden Olive

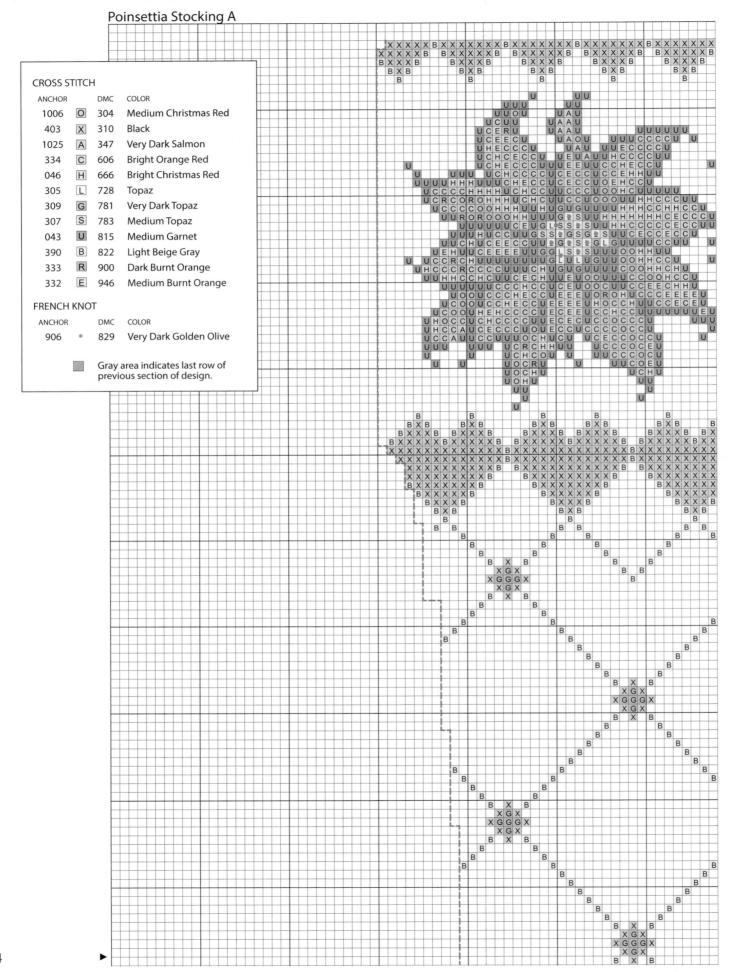

CROSS STITCH

ANCHOR		DMC	COLOR
1006	O	304	Medium Christmas Red
403	X	310	Black
1025	A	347	Very Dark Salmon
334	C	606	Bright Orange Red
046	H	666	Bright Christmas Red
305	L	728	Topaz
309	G	781	Very Dark Topaz
307	S	783	Medium Topaz
043	U	815	Medium Garnet
390	B	822	Light Beige Gray
333	R	900	Dark Burnt Orange
332	E	946	Medium Burnt Orange

FRENCH KNOT

ANCHOR		DMC	COLOR
906	•	829	Very Dark Golden Olive

Gray area indicates last row of previous section of design.

▼ Poinsettia Stocking B

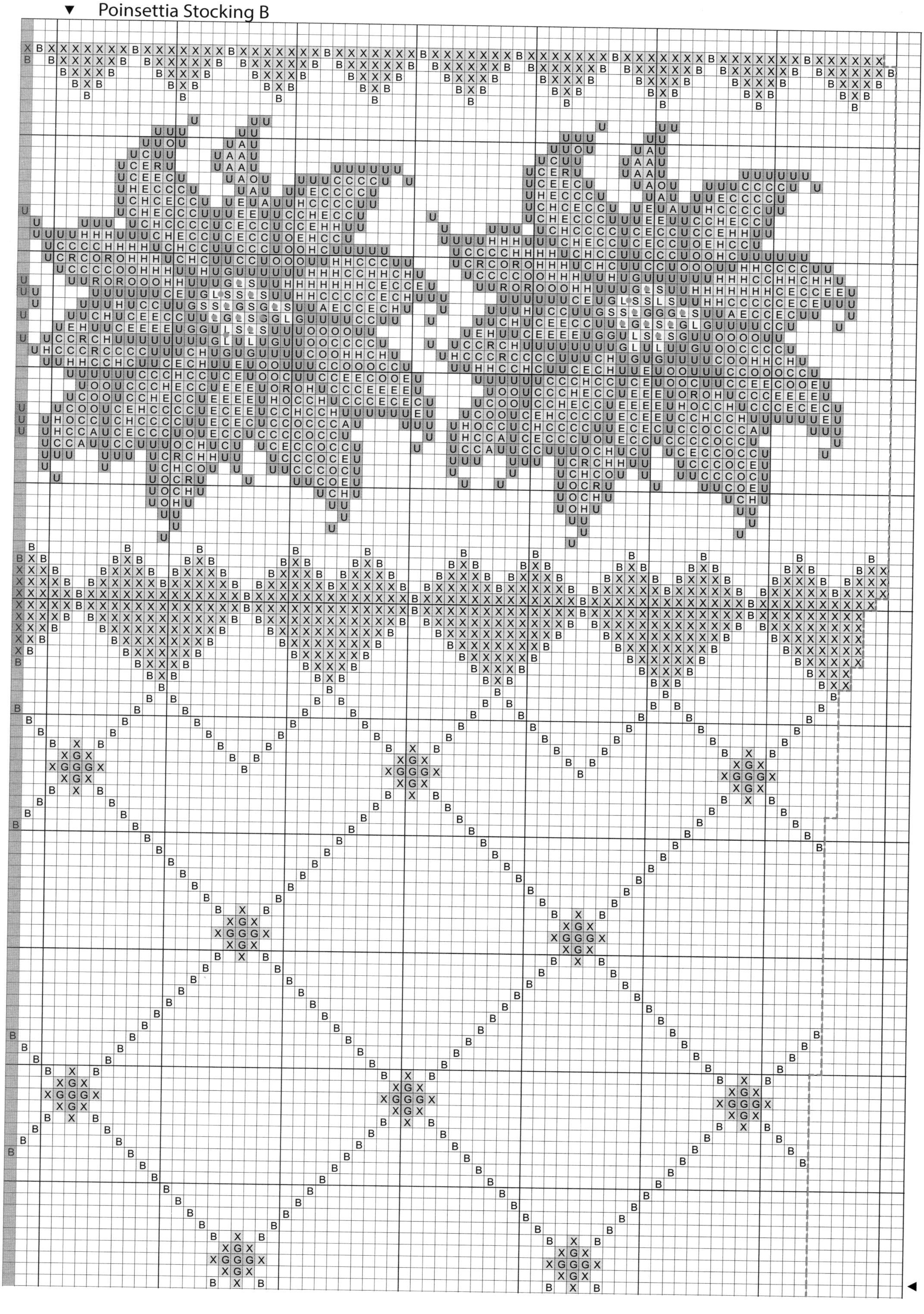

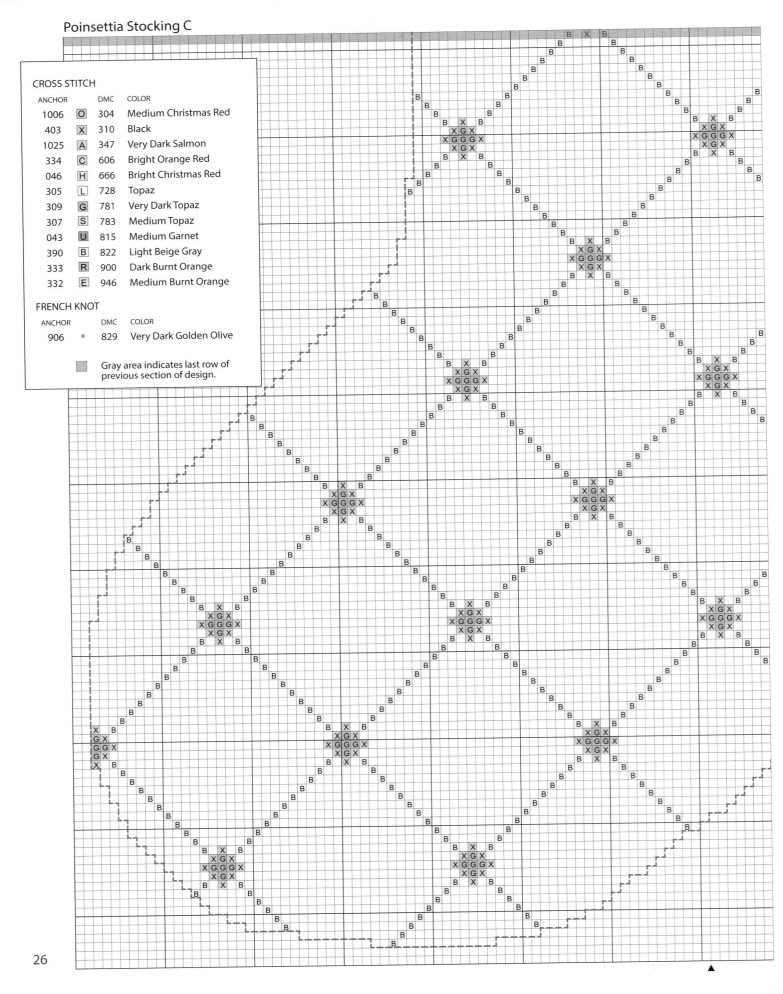

CROSS STITCH

ANCHOR		DMC	COLOR
1006	O	304	Medium Christmas Red
403	X	310	Black
1025	A	347	Very Dark Salmon
334	C	606	Bright Orange Red
046	H	666	Bright Christmas Red
305	L	728	Topaz
309	G	781	Very Dark Topaz
307	S	783	Medium Topaz
043	U	815	Medium Garnet
390	B	822	Light Beige Gray
333	R	900	Dark Burnt Orange
332	E	946	Medium Burnt Orange

FRENCH KNOT

ANCHOR		DMC	COLOR
906	•	829	Very Dark Golden Olive

Gray area indicates last row of previous section of design.

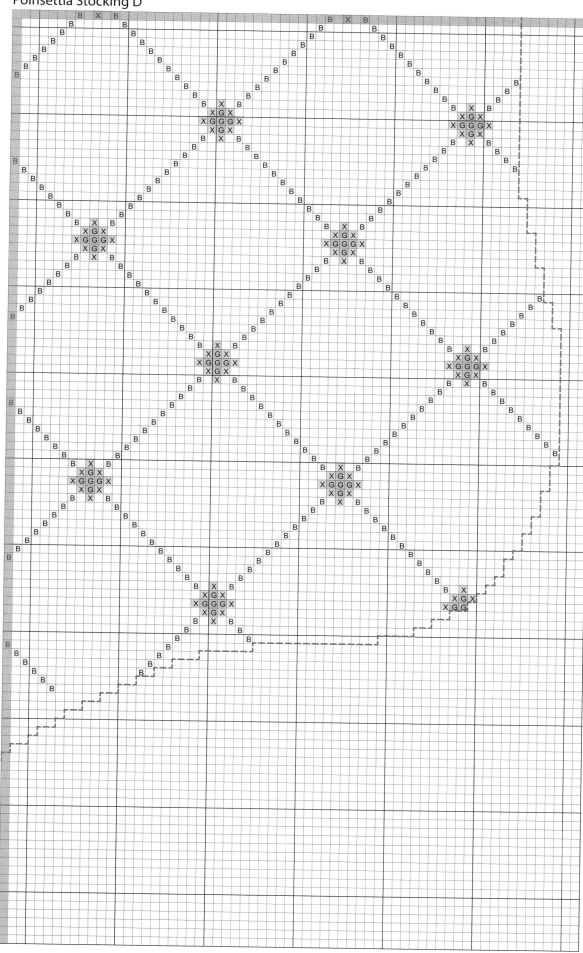

Angelic Pets Stocking

Remember your furry friends this Christmas with these adorable stockings! Percy and Bruno are absolutely angelic in their gingham gowns with fish and bone trim. Personalize the stockings with your favorite pets' names for the purr-fect gift!

Designed by Barbara Sestok

Stitch Count (each design) = 78w × 115h

FABRIC SIZE

- One 14" × 16" (35.6cm × 40.6cm) piece of 28-ct. Light Blue Jobelan® by Wichelt Imports (stitched over two threads) for each stocking
- One 12" × 8" (30.5cm × 20.3cm) piece of 28-ct. White Jobelan by Wichelt Imports (stitched over two threads) for each stocking cuff

Note: On the models shown, the cuffs were stitched separately on white needlework fabric. To stitch as one piece, only the light blue fabric is needed.

DESIGN SIZE (each design)

- 28-ct. = 5½" × 8¼" (14.0cm × 21.0cm)

FINISHING MATERIALS

- One 12" × 14" piece of 28-ct. Light Blue Jobelan for each stocking backing
- One 12" × 8" piece of 28-ct. White Jobelan for each cuff backing (if cuff is stitched separately)
- One 6" length of coordinating twisted cording for hanger
- Matching sewing thread

GENERAL INSTRUCTIONS

Center the design on the Light Blue fabric and begin stitching over two fabric threads (if stitching the cuff separately, stitch it on the White fabric over two threads). Work cross stitches with two strands of cotton or metallic embroidery floss. Use one strand of cotton embroidery floss to work French knots, wrapping the floss twice around the needle. Work backstitches with one strand of cotton or metallic embroidery floss. Stitch the pet's name using the alphabet below and the floss colors indicated on each chart. Use a pressing cloth to carefully iron the needlework from the back before finishing.

FINISHING INSTRUCTIONS

Enlarge the stocking template by 200% on a copy machine. Trace the stocking template onto the back of the stitched piece, centering the design from left to right and about ¾" from the bottom. Use the template to trace and cut out the back panel from the other piece of Light Blue fabric. Trim the stitched cuff, leaving 1" of unstitched fabric above and below the design, and ½" on both sides.

Cut a piece of White fabric the same dimensions to form the back cuff piece. Fold the top and bottom of the cuff so only the stitched area shows and press in place. Fold and press the blank cuff piece in the same manner. Place the stitched cuff piece right side up on the right side of the stitched stocking panel, aligning the top of the cuff's stitching with the top of the stocking, and fold the cuff top over to the back of the stocking. Pin in place.

Repeat with the back cuff piece and back stocking panel. Place the stocking panels with right sides together and pin in place. Sew together ¼" in from the edge along the sides and bottom of the stocking. Turn right side out and sew cording into a loop to create a hanger on the left inside edge of the stocking.

If stitching the stocking and cuff as one, center and trace the template on the back of the stitched piece, aligning and centering the stitched cuff area with the top of the stocking template. Cut out, adding 1" extra to the top of the stocking above the cuff. Use this piece to trace and cut the back panel from the Light Blue fabric. Fold the extra 1" at the top edge of each panel to the back and press in place. Place the stocking panels with right sides together and pin in place. Sew together ¼" in from the edge along the sides and bottom of the stocking. Turn right side out and sew cording into a loop to create a hanger on the left inside edge of the stocking.

CROSS STITCH

ANCHOR		DMC	COLOR
002	·	White	White
403	X	310	Black
358	E	433	Medium Brown
256	J	704	Bright Chartreuse
326	F	720	Dark Orange Spice
295	L	726	Light Topaz
304	S	741	Medium Tangerine
275	G	746	Off White
259	M	772	Very Light Yellow Green
024	P	776	Medium Pink
258	K	904	Very Dark Parrot Green
881	7	945	Tawny
355	B	975	Dark Golden Brown
397	D	3024	Very Light Brown Gray
365	Y	3826	Golden Brown
029	H	3831	Dark Raspberry
026	N	3833	Light Raspberry
177	R	3838	Dark Lavender Blue
117	C	3840	Light Lavender Blue

DMC LIGHT EFFECTS		COLOR
E3821	V	Light Gold

FRENCH KNOT

ANCHOR		DMC	COLOR
002	•	White	White
403	•	310	Black

BACKSTITCH

ANCHOR		DMC	COLOR
002	——	White	White
403	——	310	Black
218	——	319	Very Dark Pistachio Green
401	——	413	Dark Pewter Gray
897	——	902	Very Dark Garnet
258	——	904	Very Dark Parrot Green
029	——	3831	Dark Raspberry

DMC LIGHT EFFECTS		COLOR
E3821	——	Light Gold

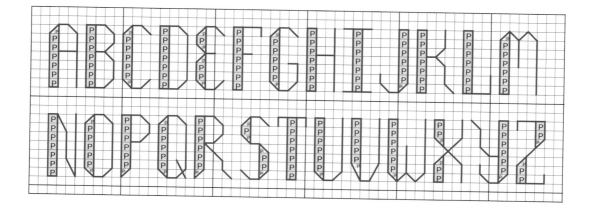

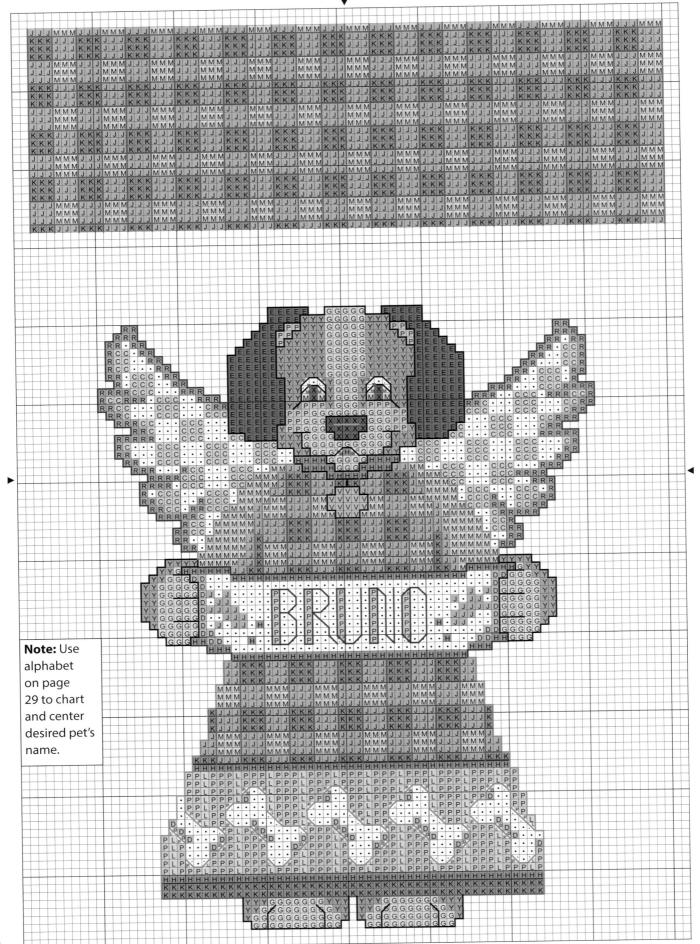

Note: Use alphabet on page 29 to chart and center desired pet's name.

Note: Cuff may be stitched separately (see page 29).

Note: Color key can be found on page 29.

Note: Use alphabet on page 29 to chart and center desired pet's name.

Note: Cuff may be stitched separately (see page 29).

Note: Color key can be found on page 29.

General Instructions

Getting Started

For most projects, the starting point is at the center. Every chart has arrows that indicate the horizontal and vertical centers. With your finger, trace along the grid to the point where the two centers meet. Compare a symbol at the center of the chart to the key and choose which floss color to stitch first. To find the center of the fabric, fold it into quarters and finger-crease.

Cut the floss into 15" lengths and separate all six strands. Recombine the appropriate number of strands and thread them into a blunt-tip needle. Unless otherwise indicated, use two strands of floss to work cross stitches, three-quarter cross stitches, half cross stitches, and quarter cross stitches. Use one strand of floss to work backstitches and French knots.

To Secure Thread at the Beginning

The most common way to secure the beginning tail of the thread is to hold it on the wrong side of the fabric under the first four or five stitches.

To Secure Thread at the End

To finish, slip the threaded needle under previously stitched threads on the wrong side of the fabric for four or five stitches, weaving the thread back and forth a few times. Clip the thread.

Cross Stitch

Make one cross stitch for each symbol on the chart. For horizontal rows, stitch the first diagonal of each stitch in the row. Work back across the row, completing each stitch. On linen and evenweave fabrics, work the stitches over two threads as shown in the diagram. For aida cloth, each stitch fills one square. You also can work cross stitches in the reverse direction. Remember to embroider the stitches uniformly—that is, always work the top half of each stitch in the same direction.

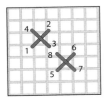

Quarter and Three-Quarter Cross Stitches

To obtain rounded shapes in a design, use quarter and three-quarter cross stitches. On linen and evenweave fabrics, a quarter stitch will extend from the corner to the center intersection of the threads. To make quarter cross stitches on aida cloth, estimate the center of the square. Three-quarter cross stitches combine a quarter cross stitch with a half cross stitch. Both stitches may slant in any direction.

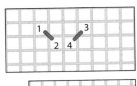

Half Cross Stitch

A half cross stitch is a single diagonal or half a cross stitch. They are indicated on the chart by a diagonal colored symbol.

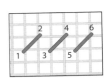

Backstitch

Bring the needle up from the back side of the fabric at odd numbers and go down at even numbers. Continue, keeping all the stitches the same length.

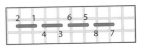

French Knot

Bring the threaded needle through the fabric and wrap the floss around the needle as shown. Tighten the twists and return the needle through the fabric in the same place. The floss will slide through the wrapped thread to make the knot.

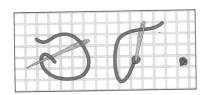

Produced by Herrschners, Inc., for distribution exclusively by Leisure Arts, Inc., 104 Champs Blvd., STE 100, Maumelle, AR 72113-6738, leisurearts.com.